MONOGRAM
Coloring Book For Adults

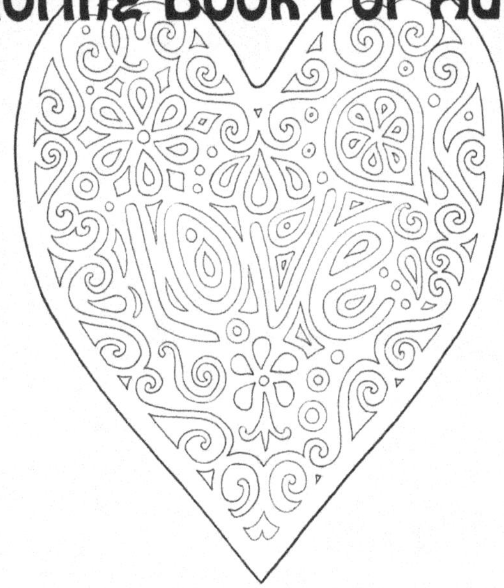

By Artist Ryan Kennedy

www.RyanKennedyArt.com

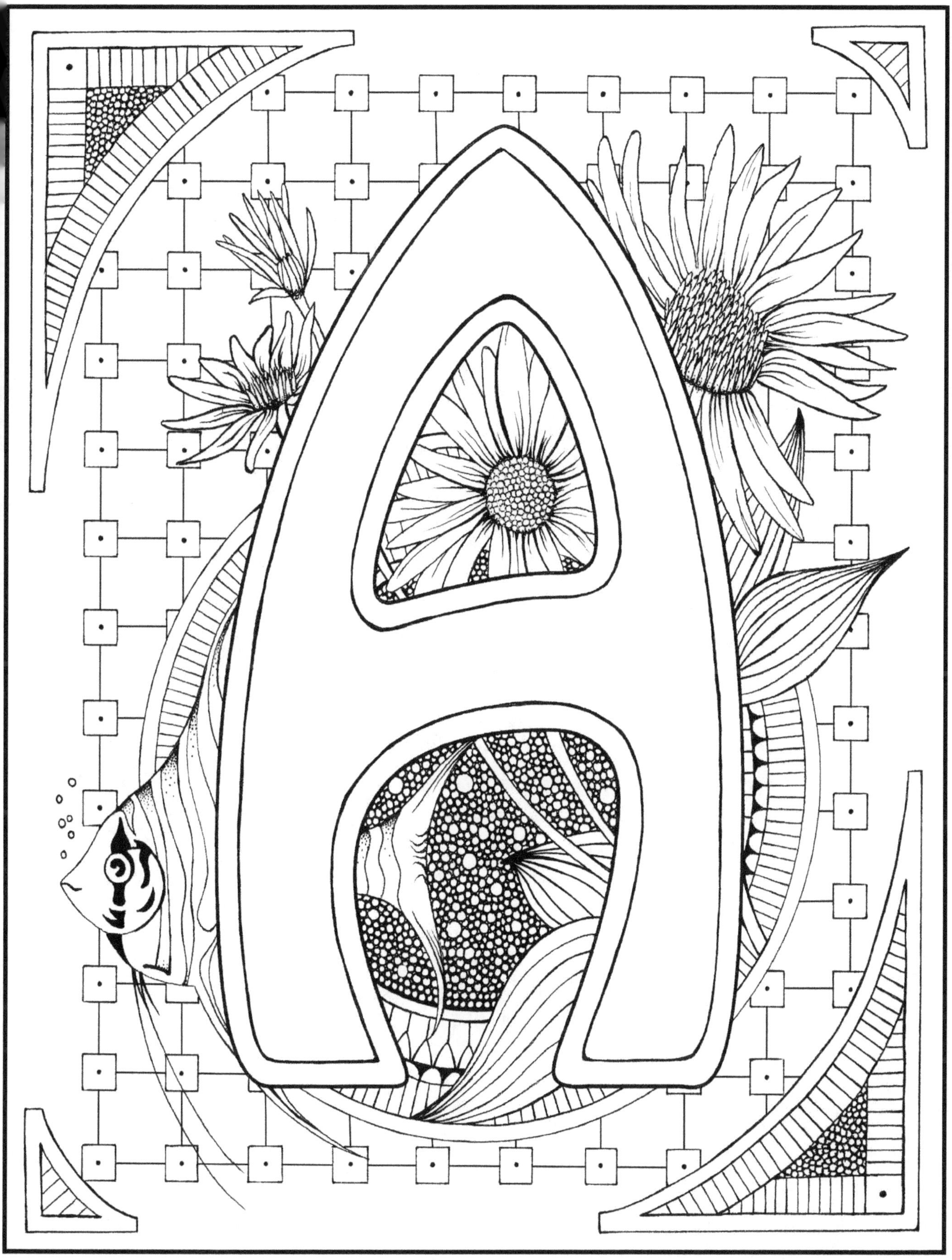

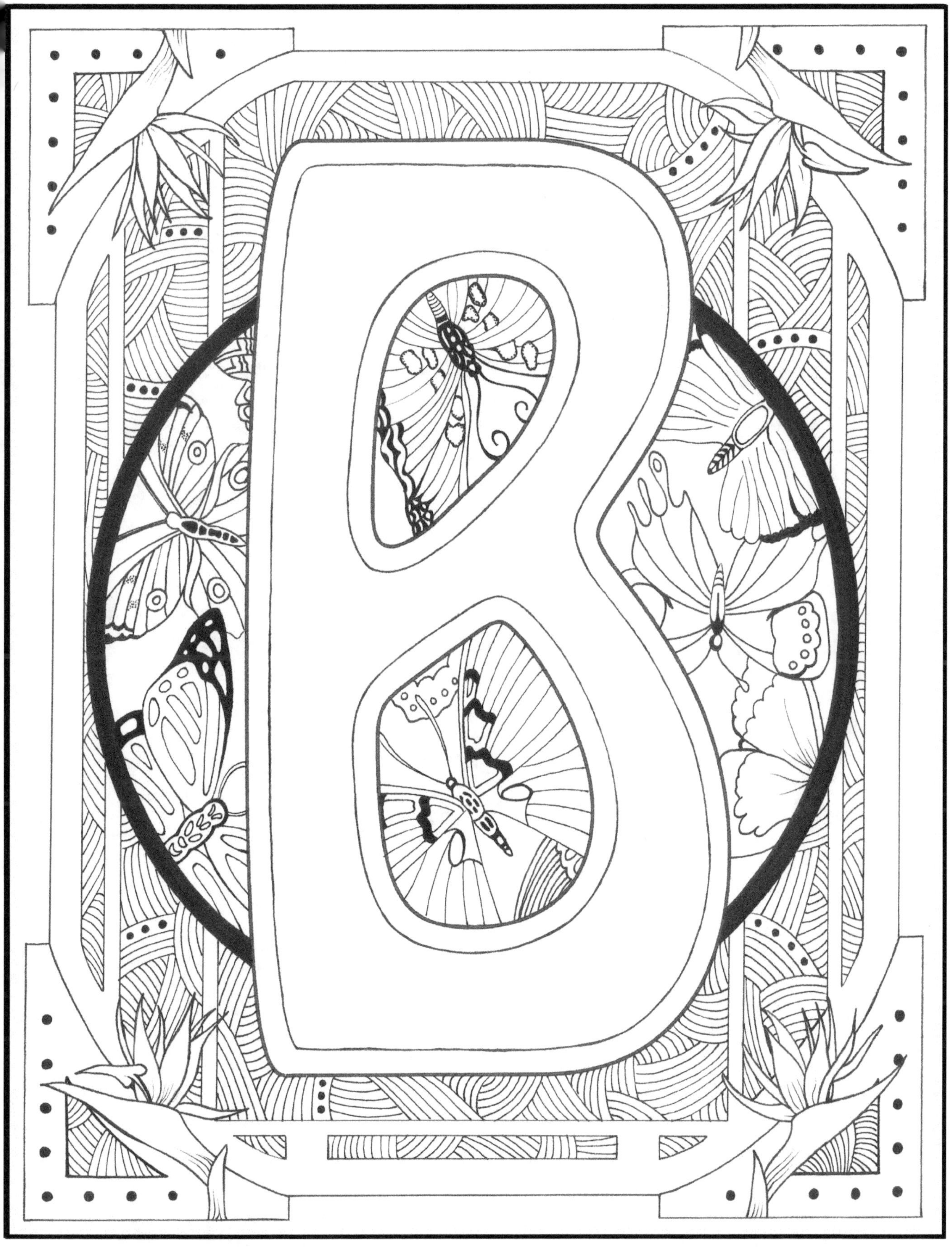

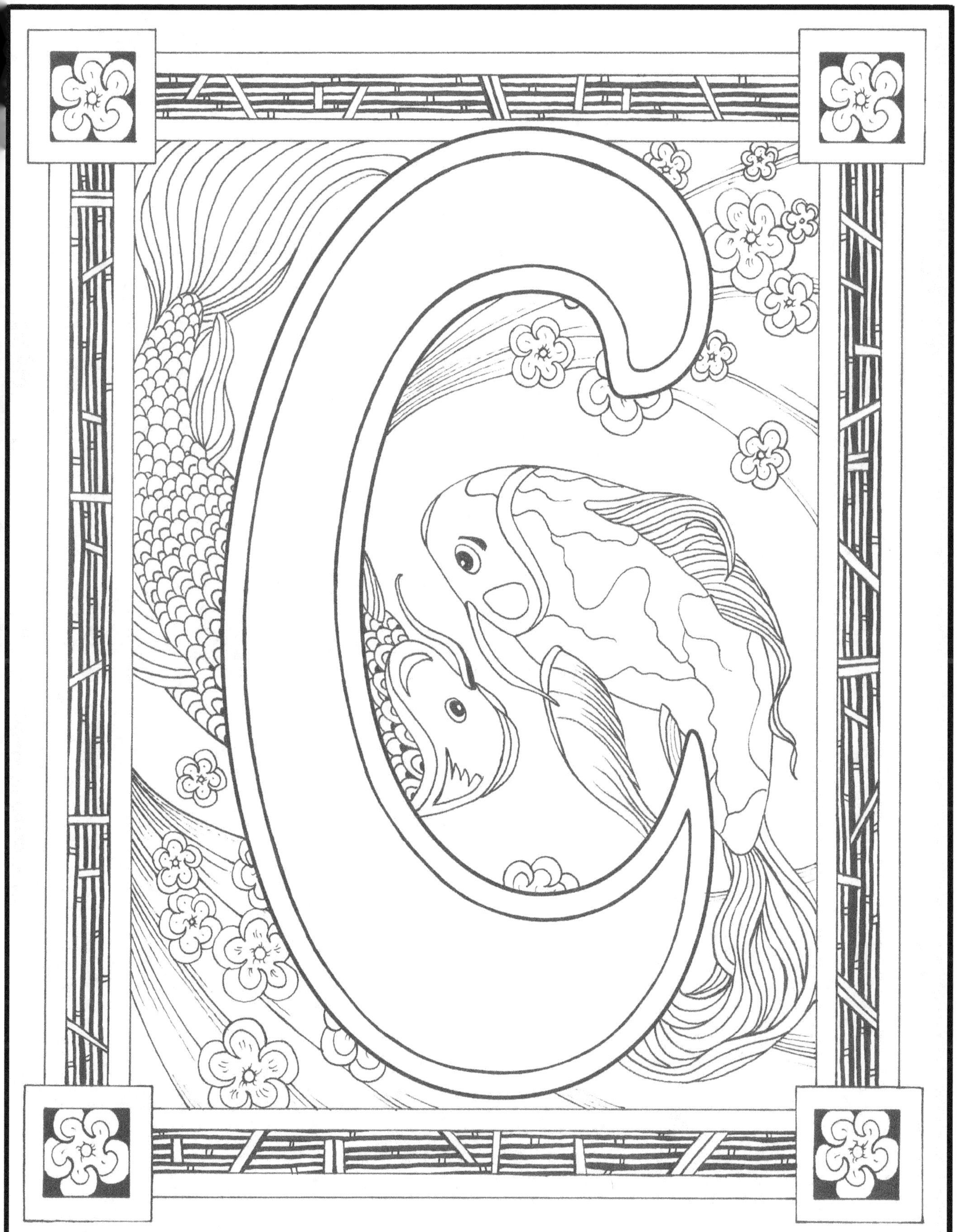

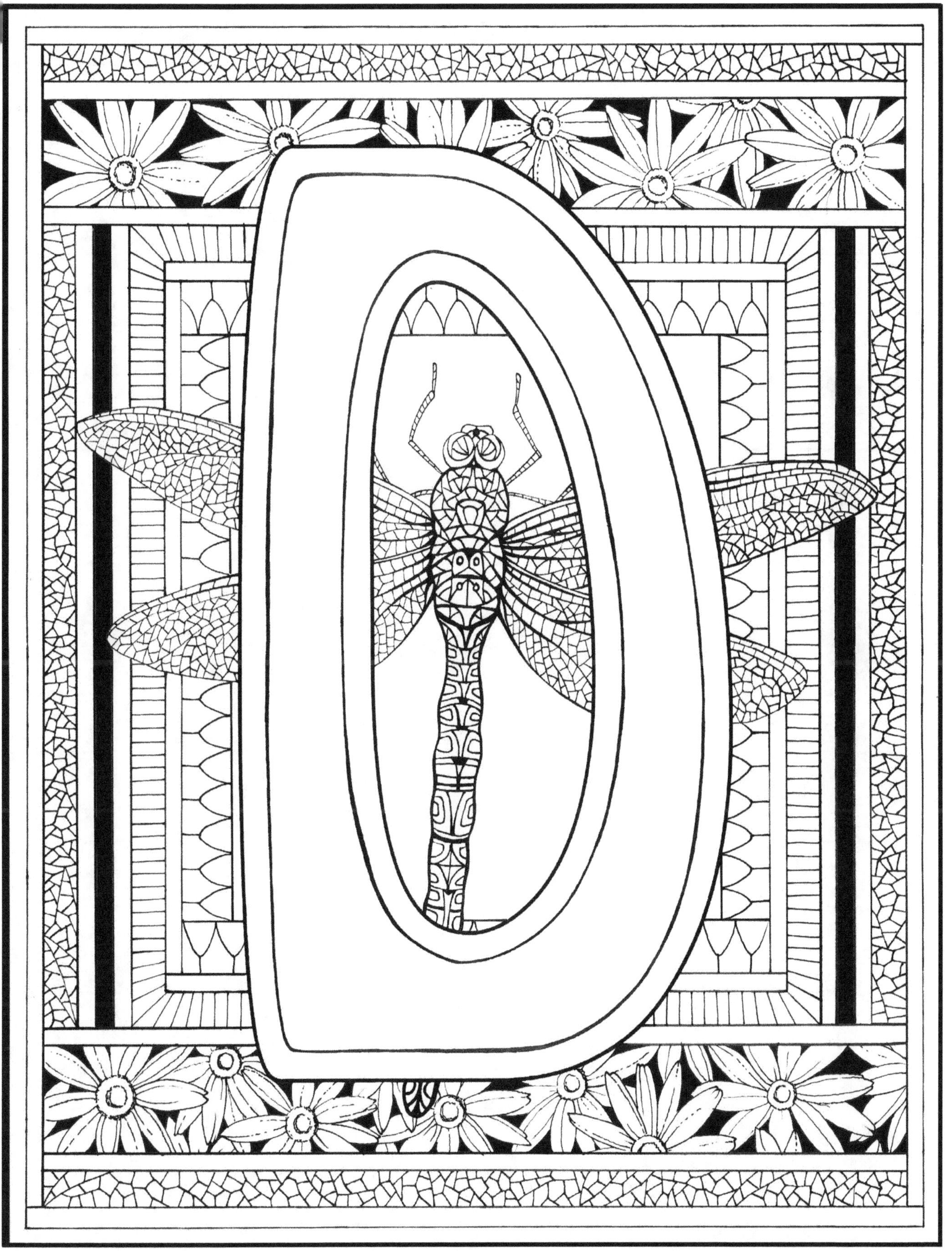

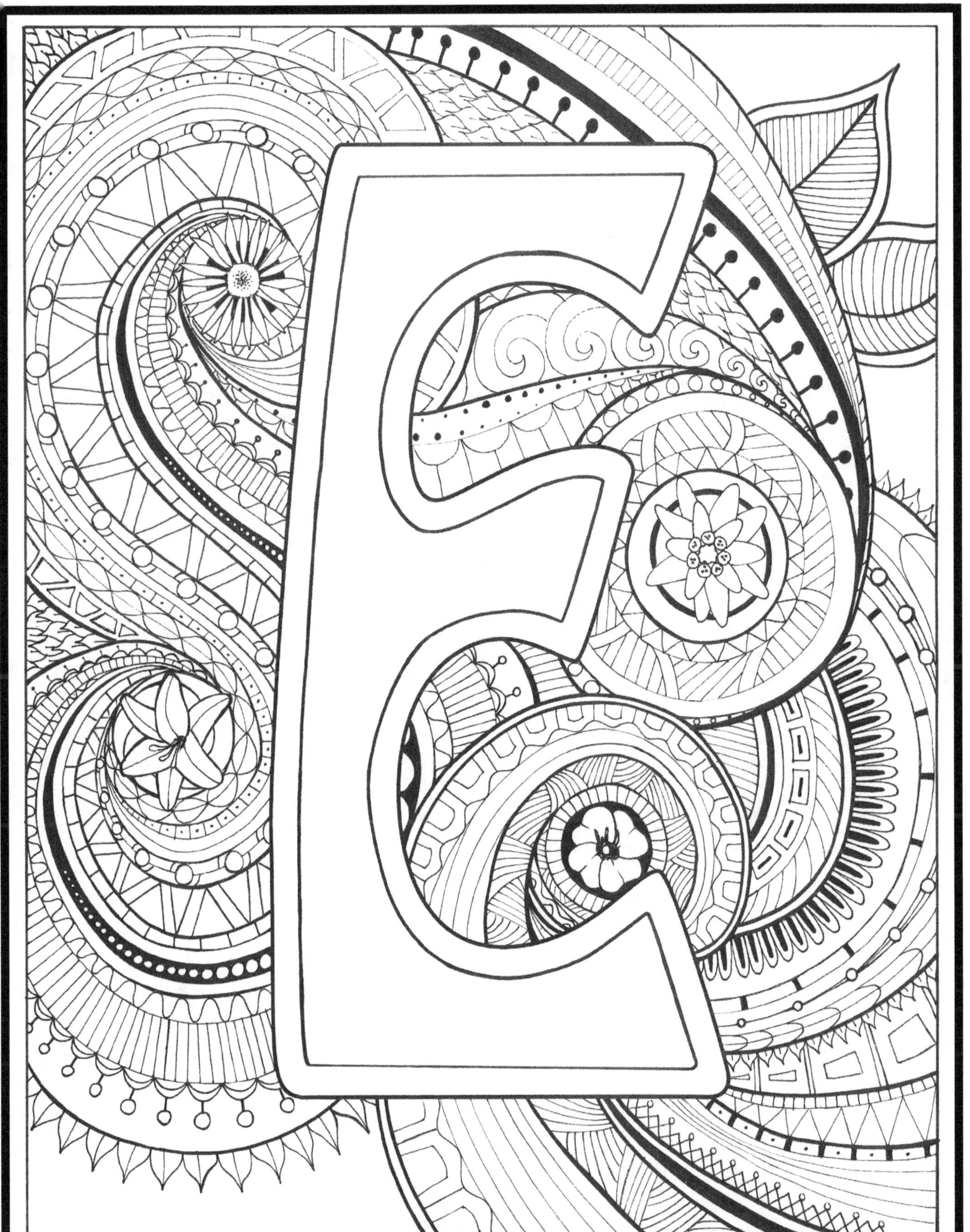

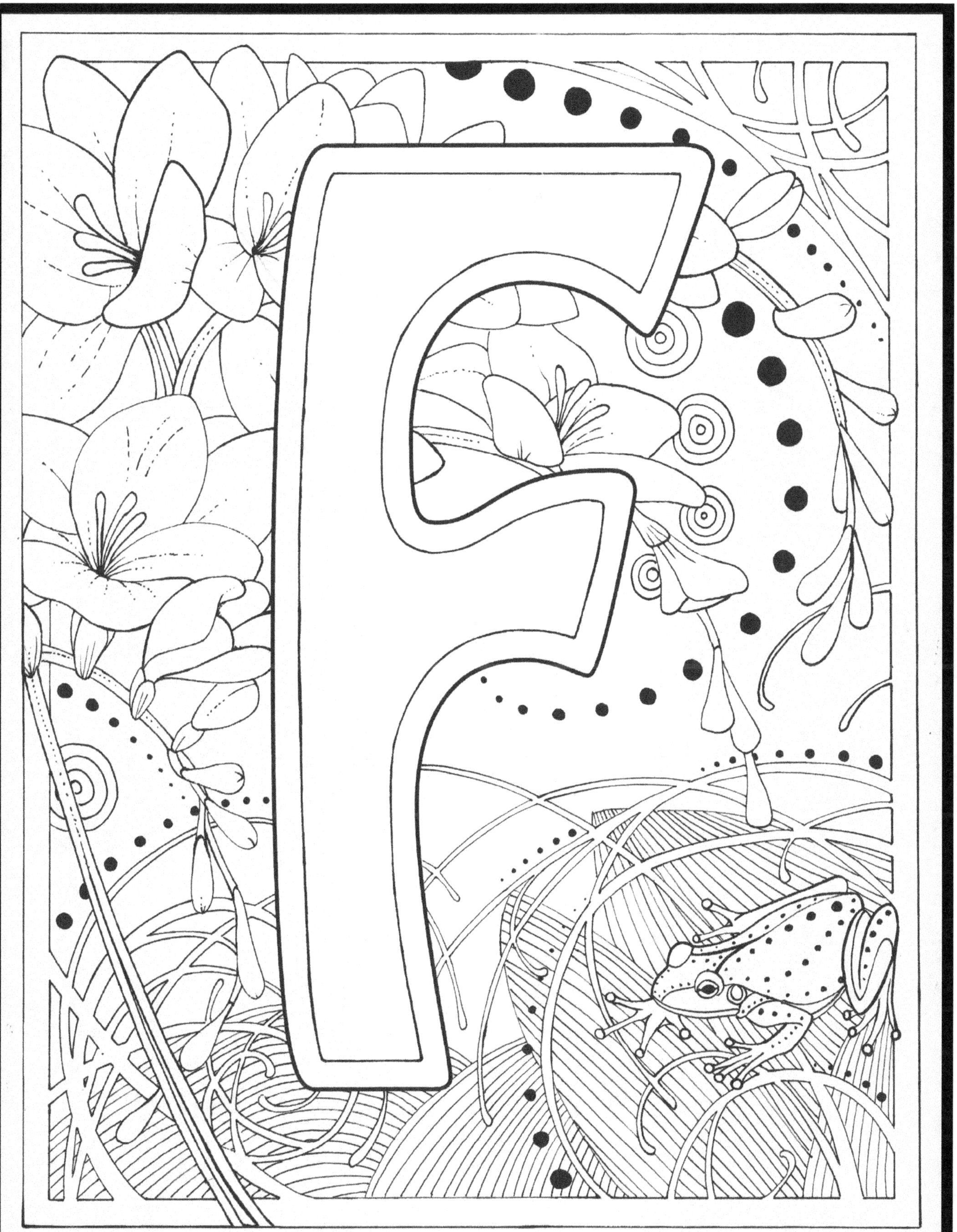

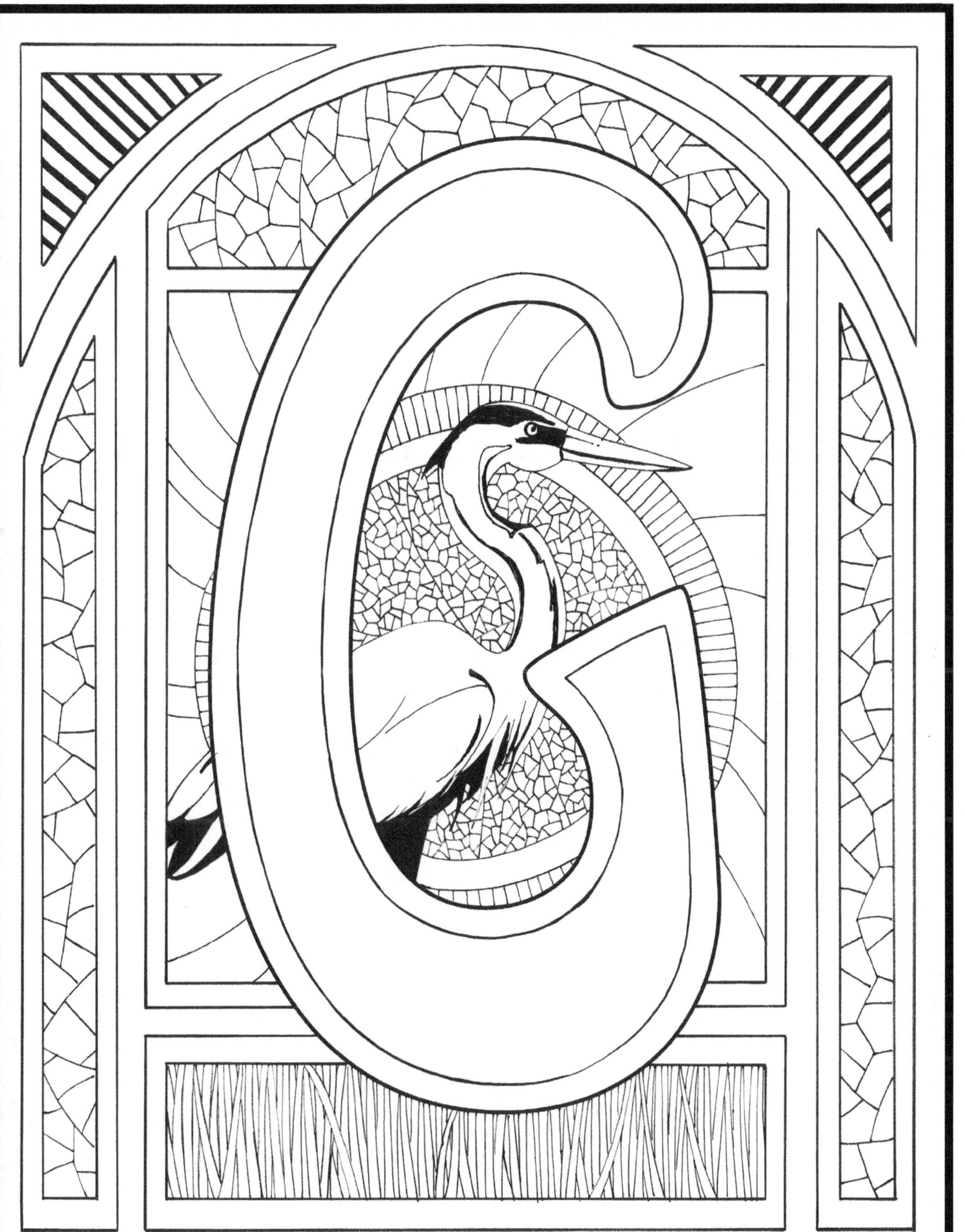

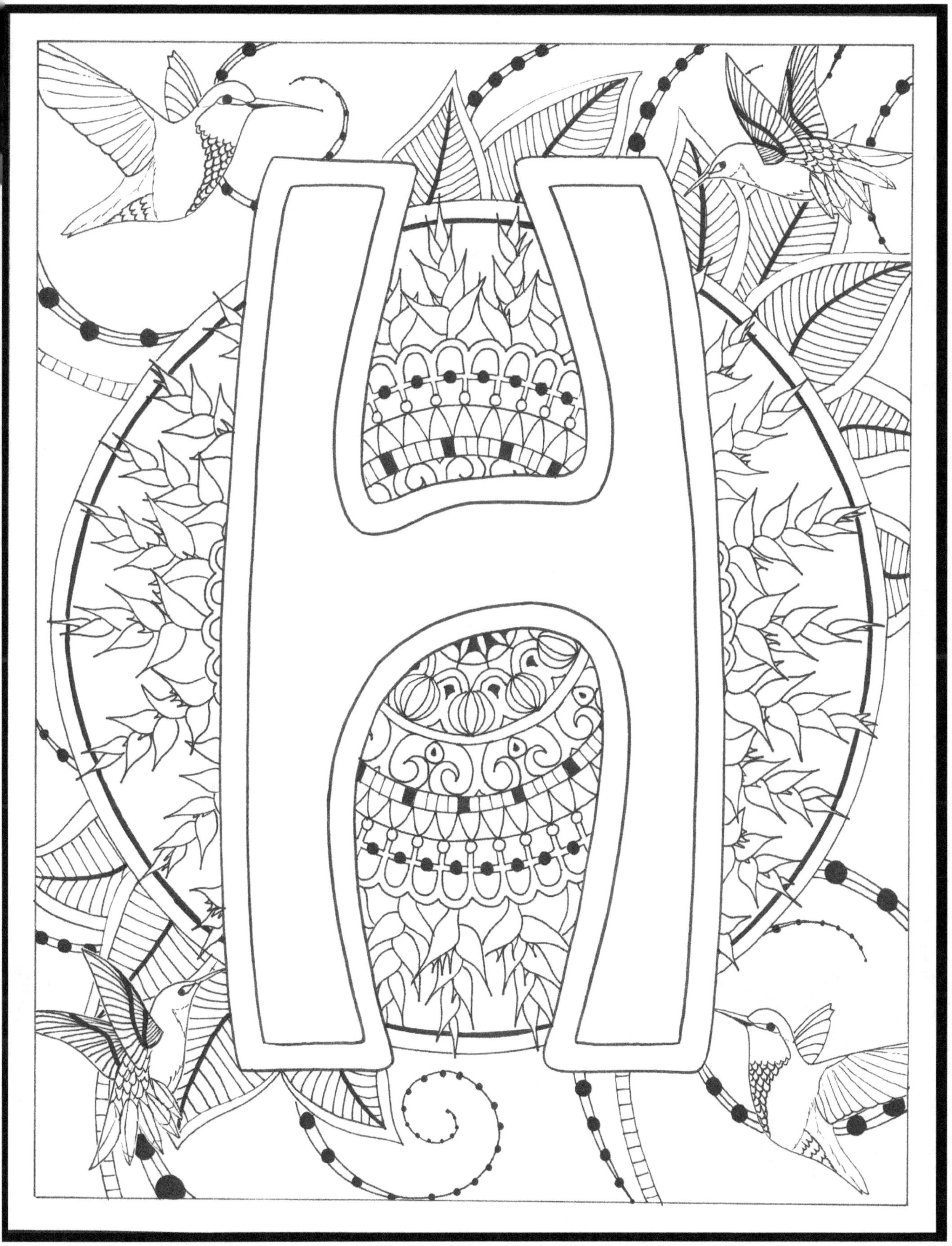

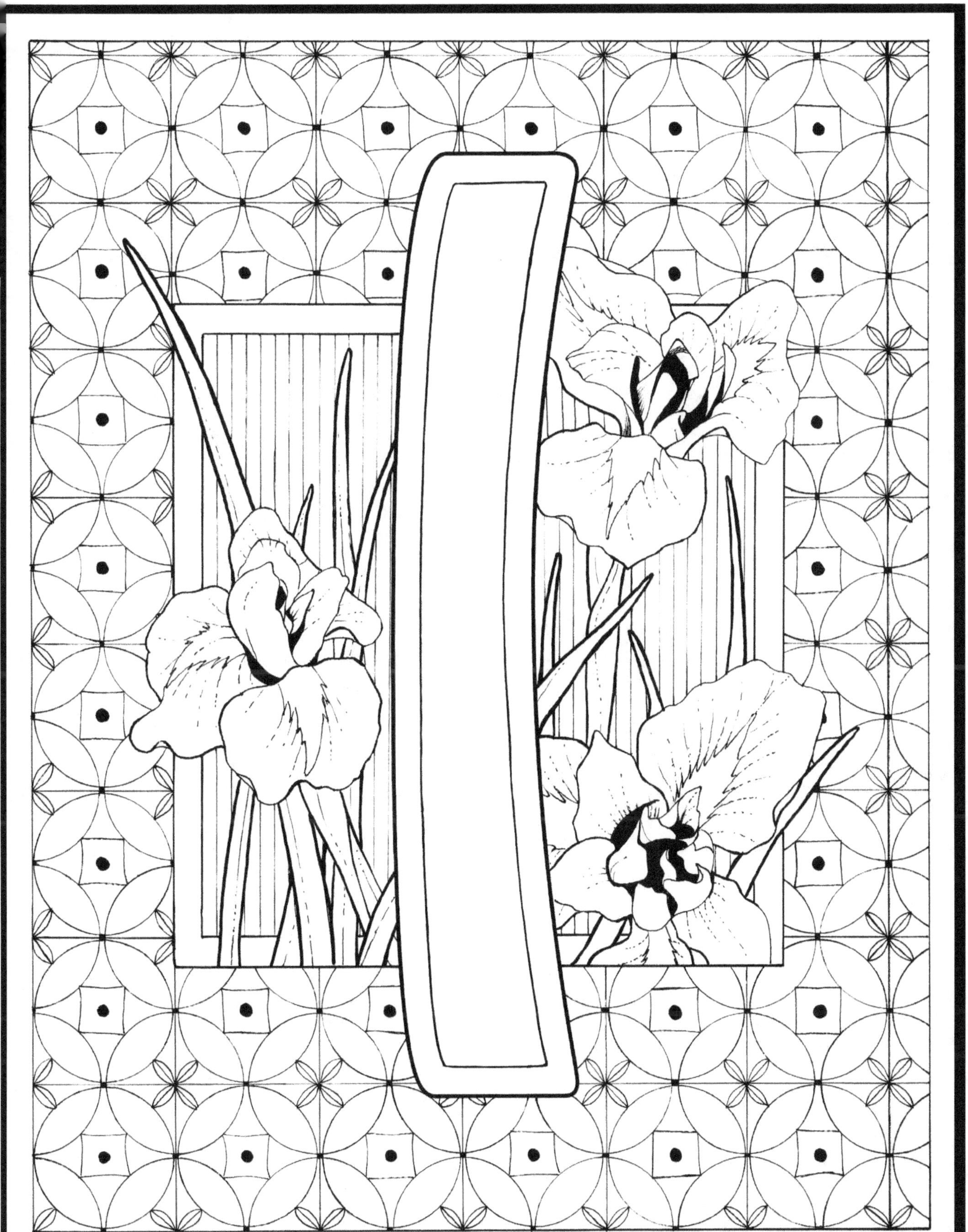

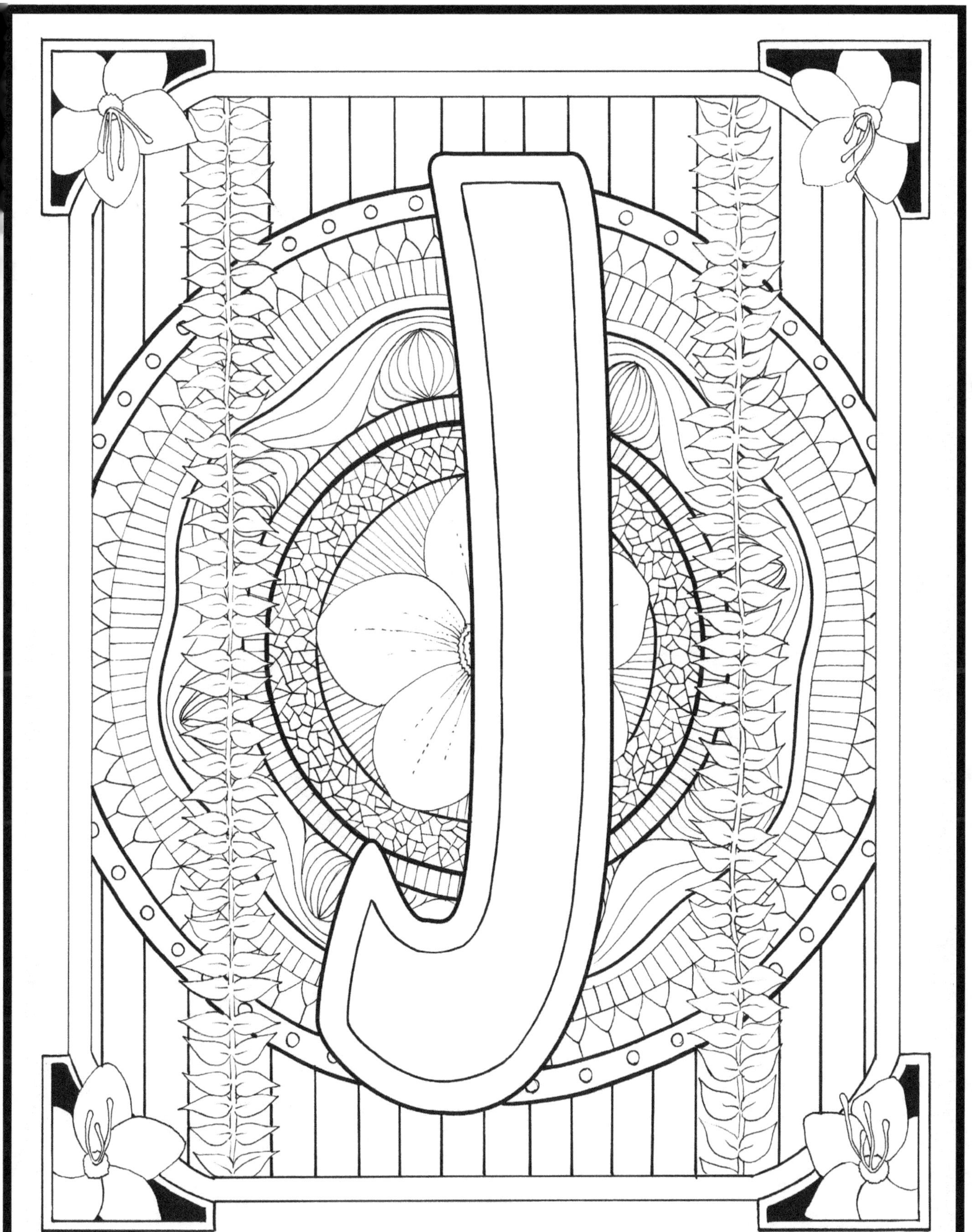

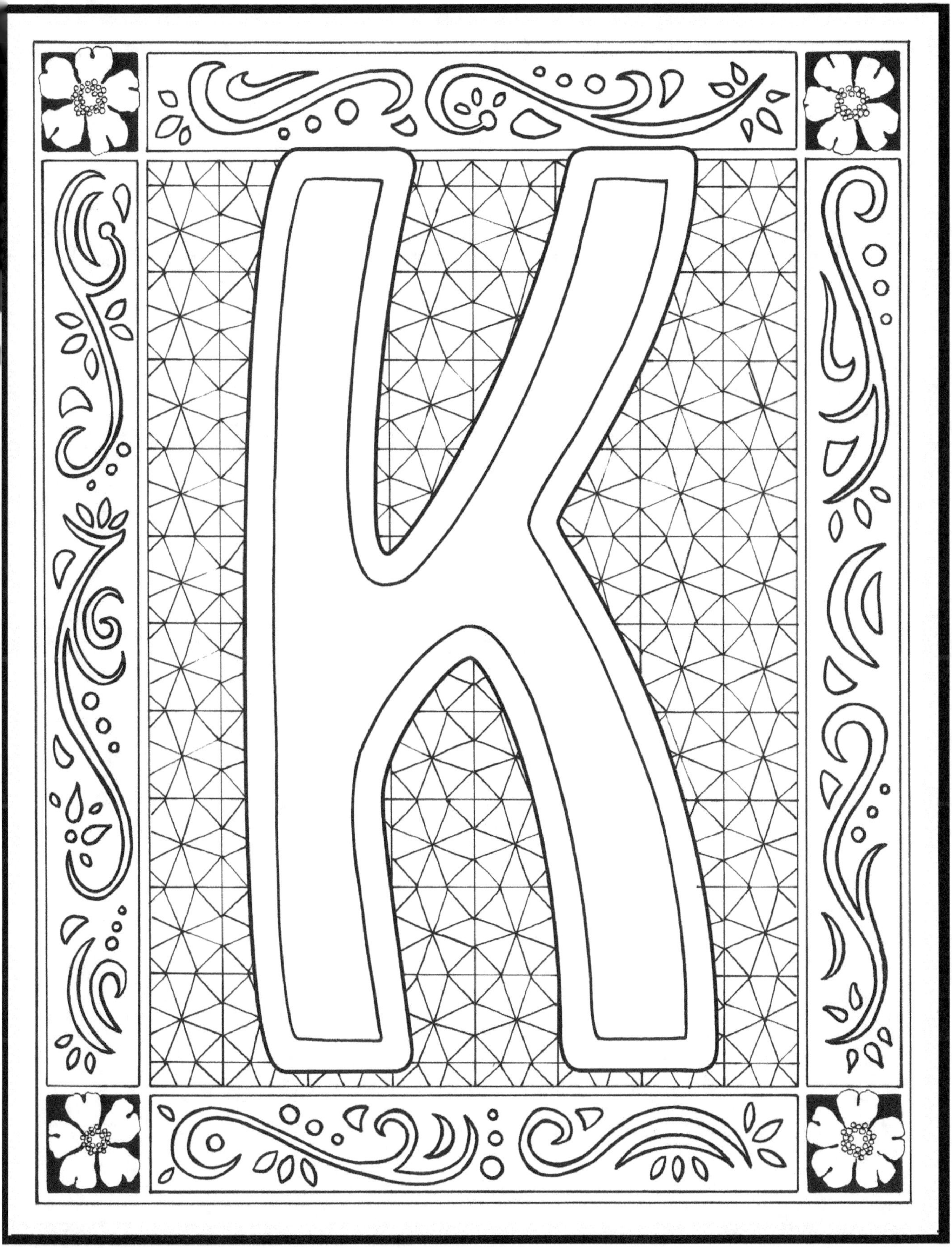
K

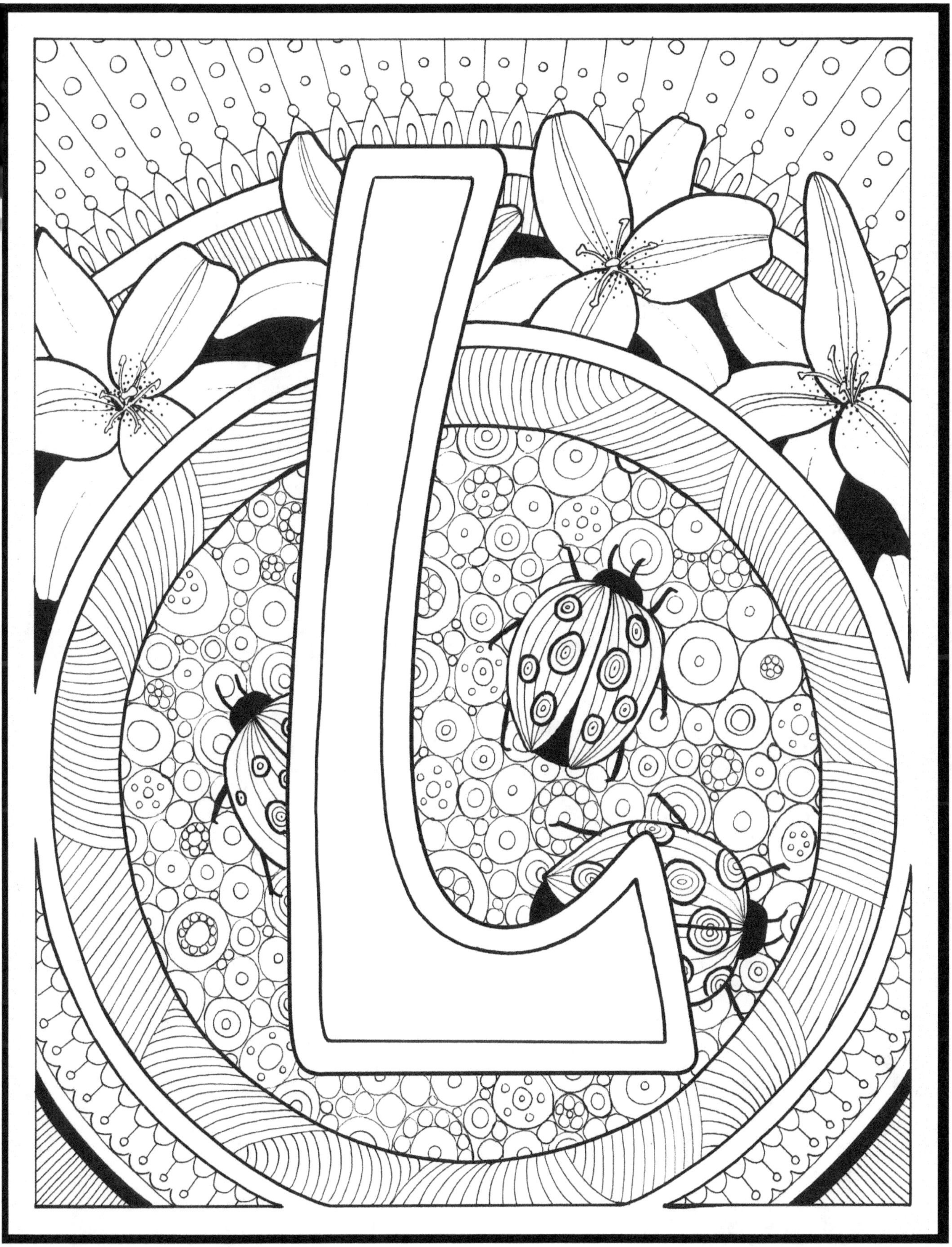

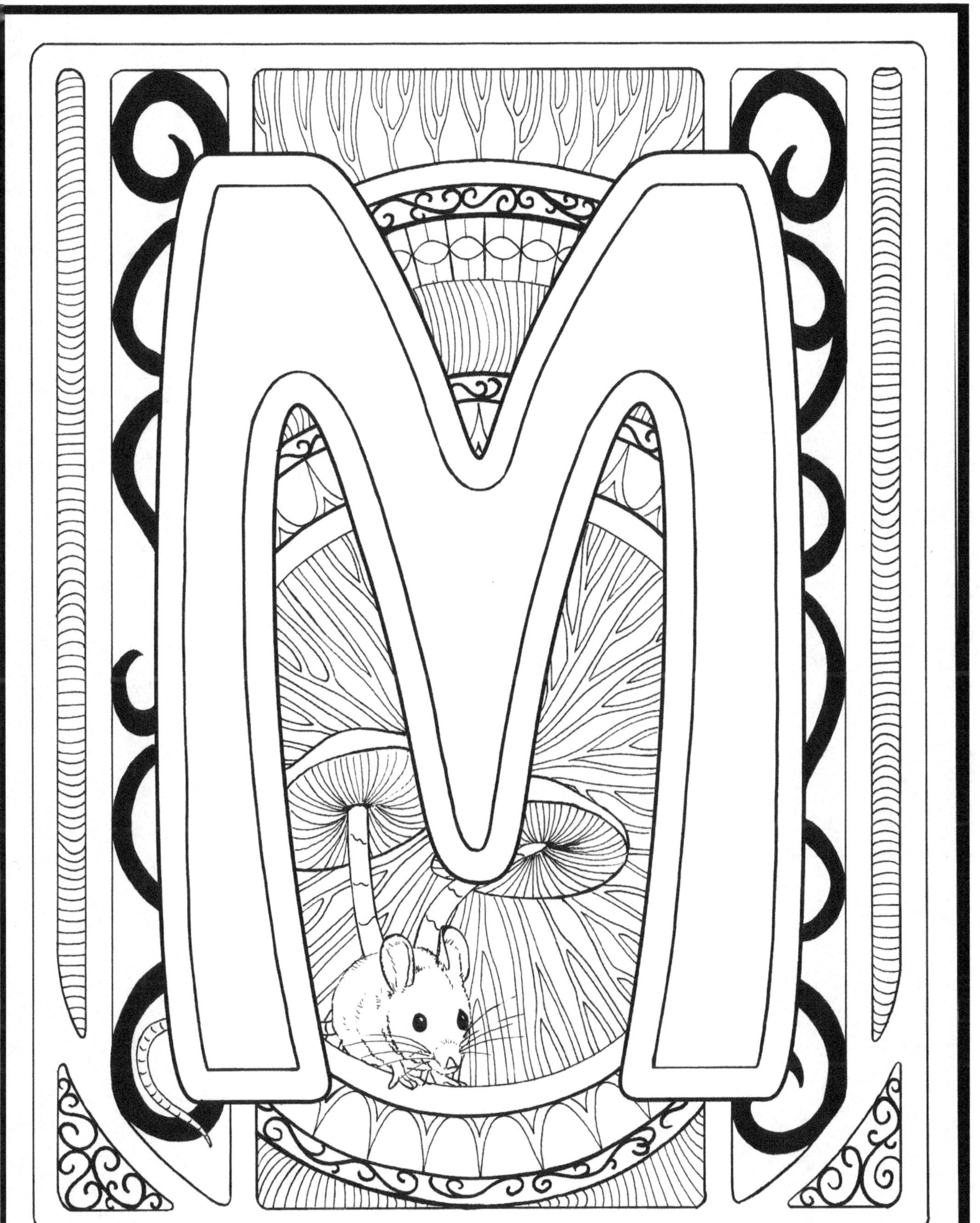

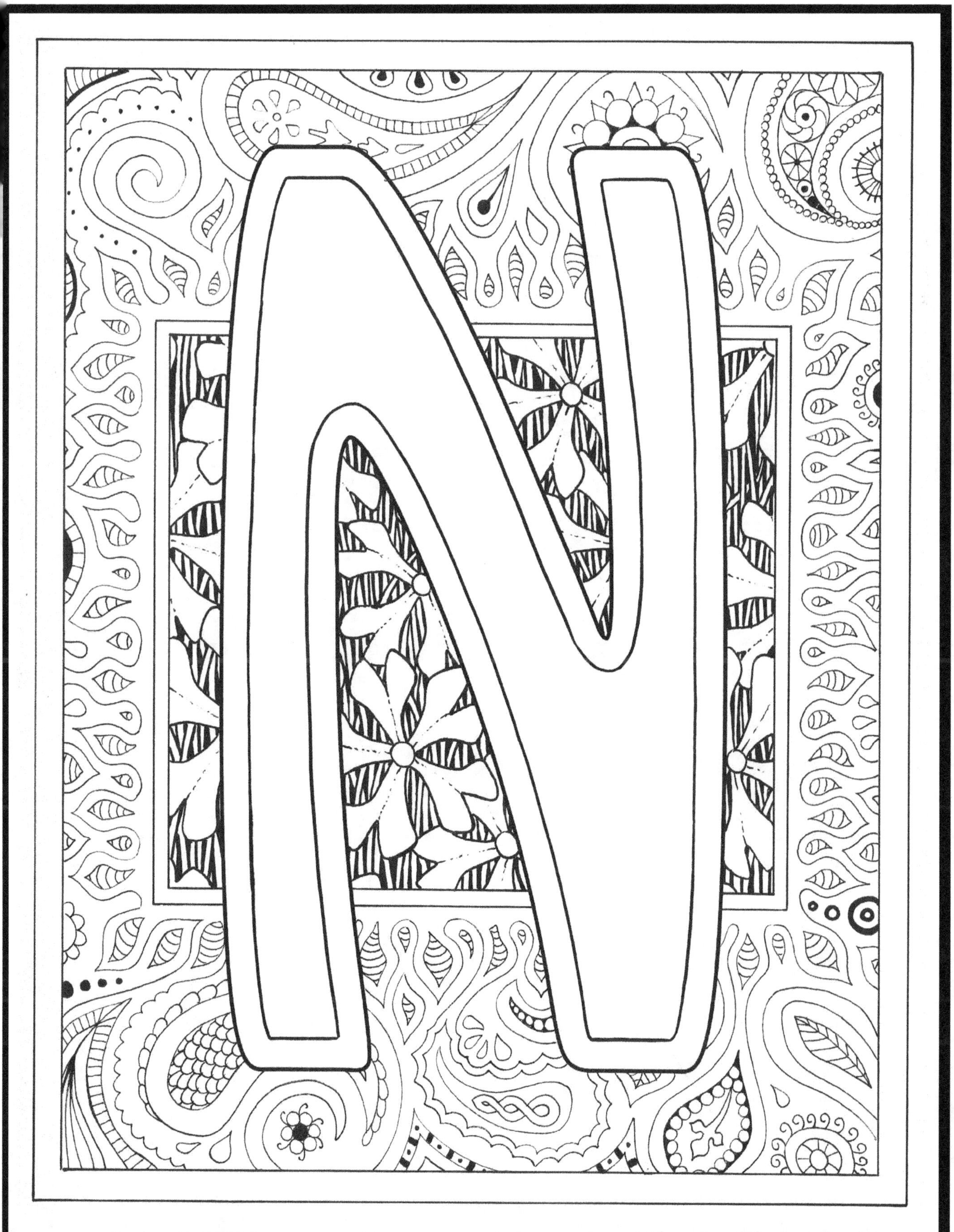
N

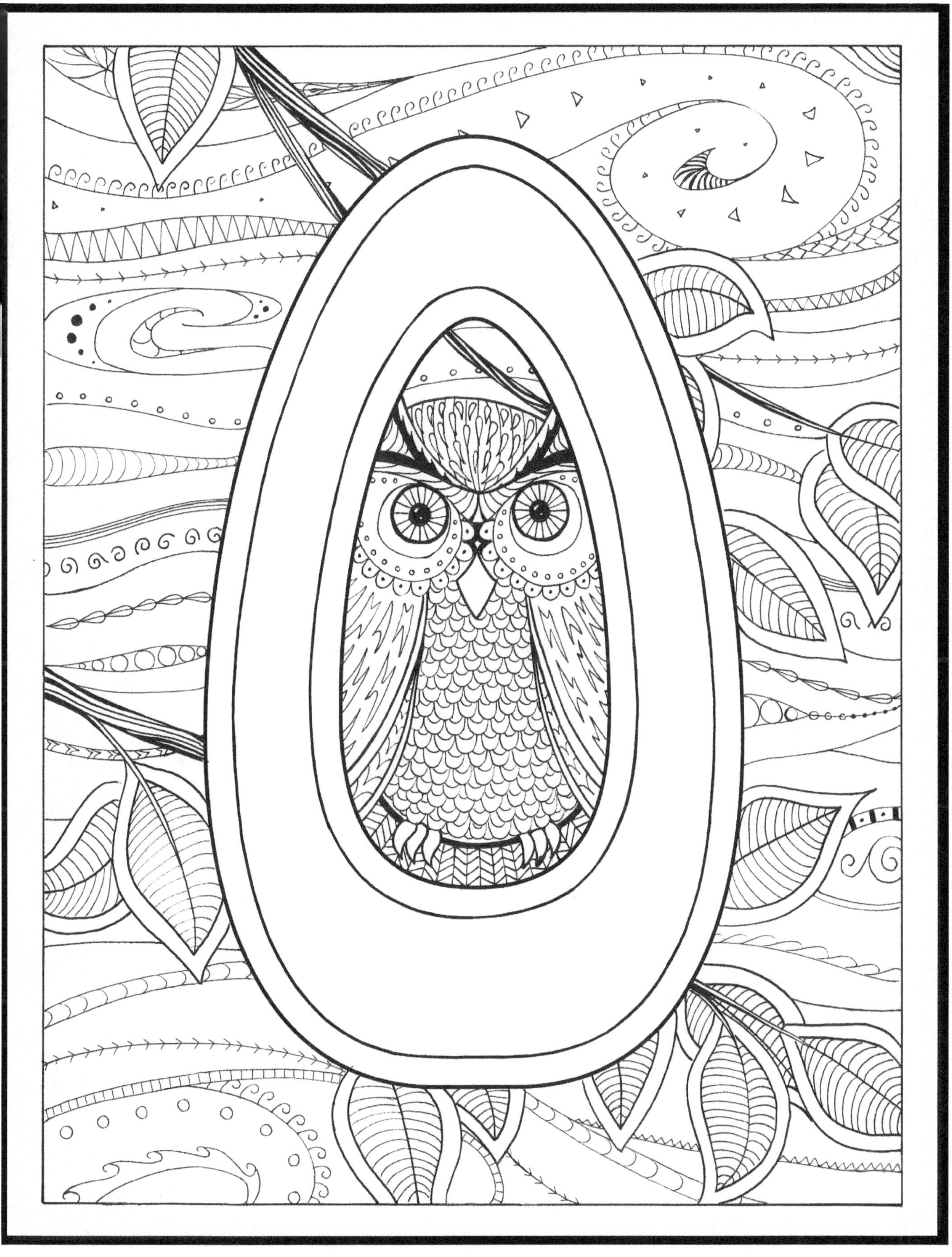

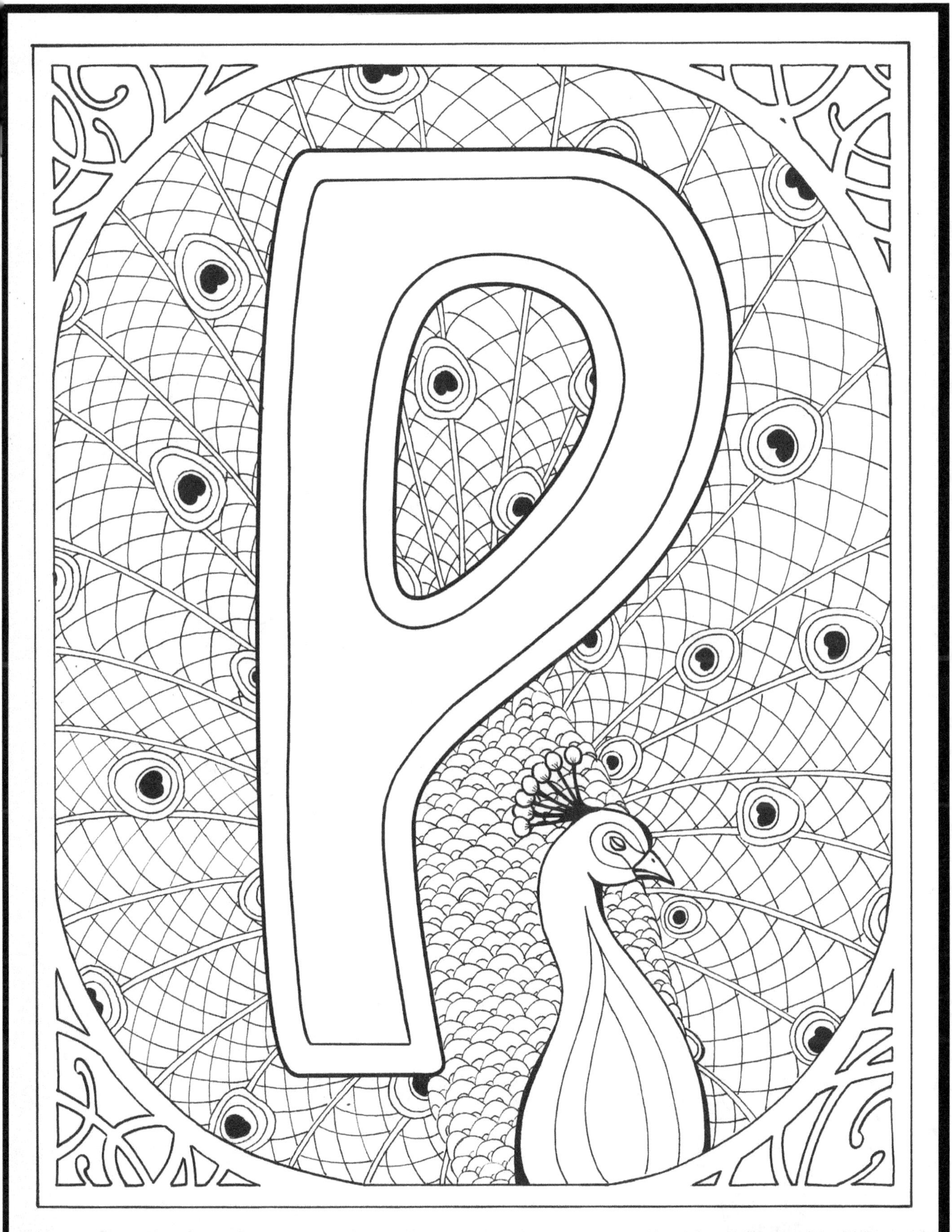

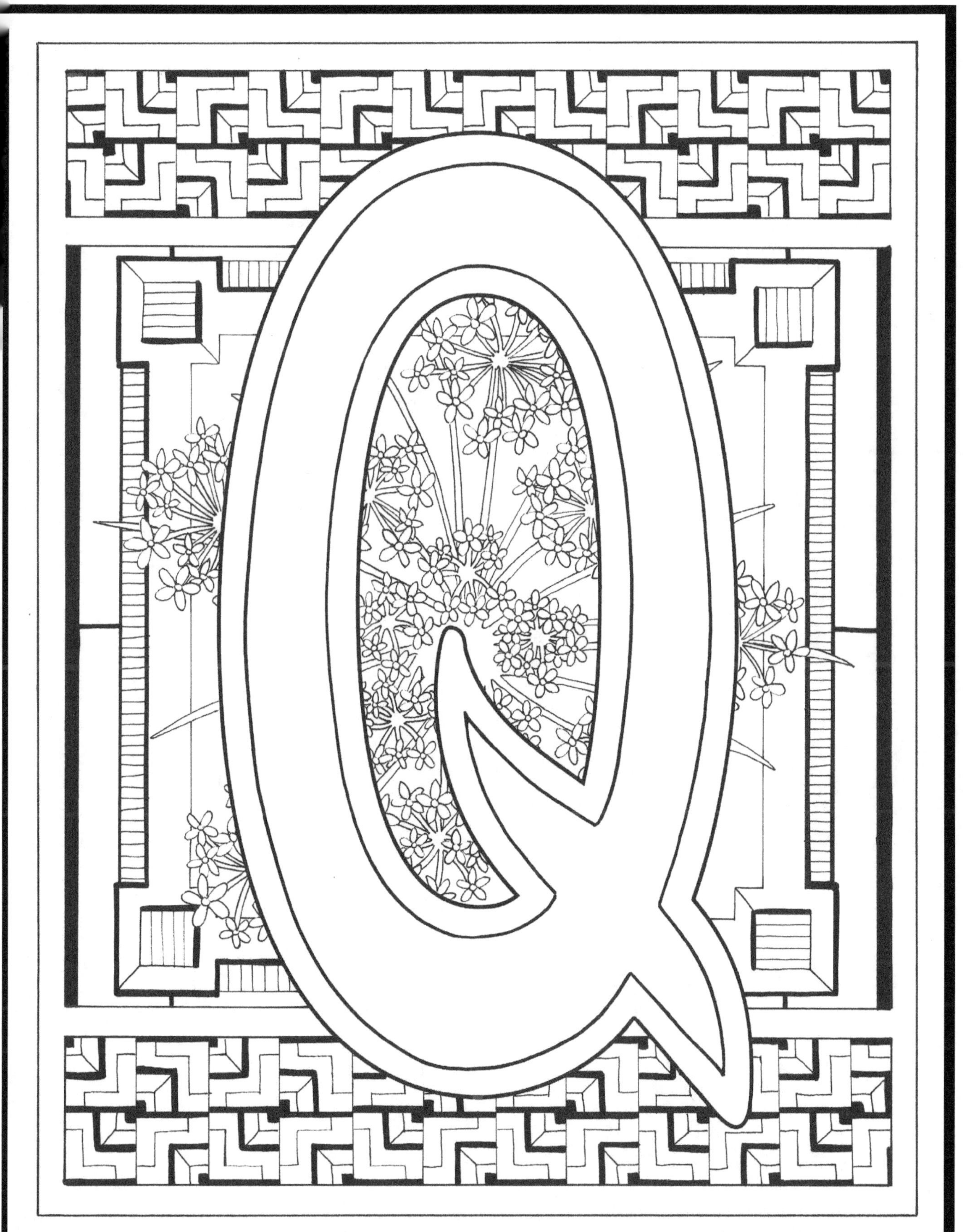

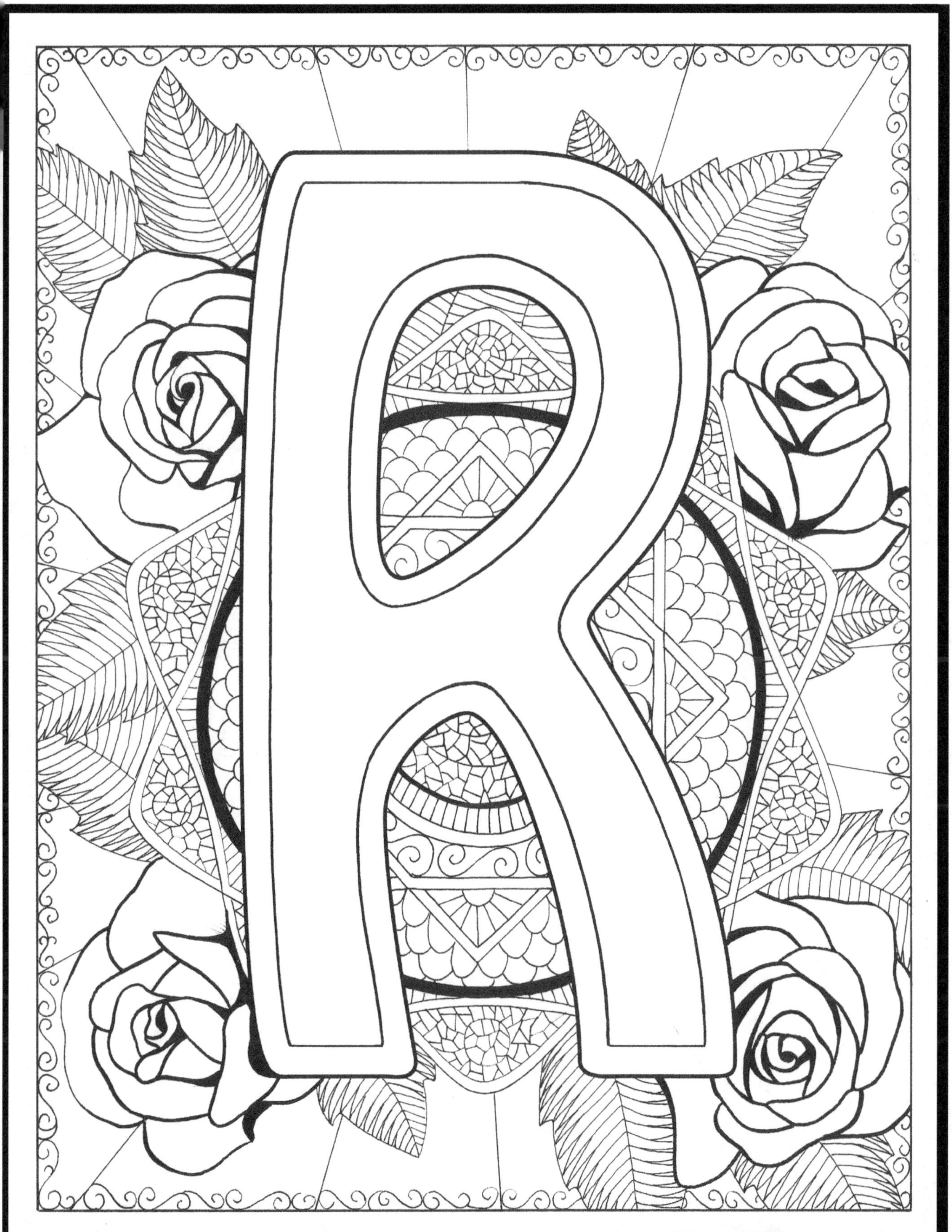

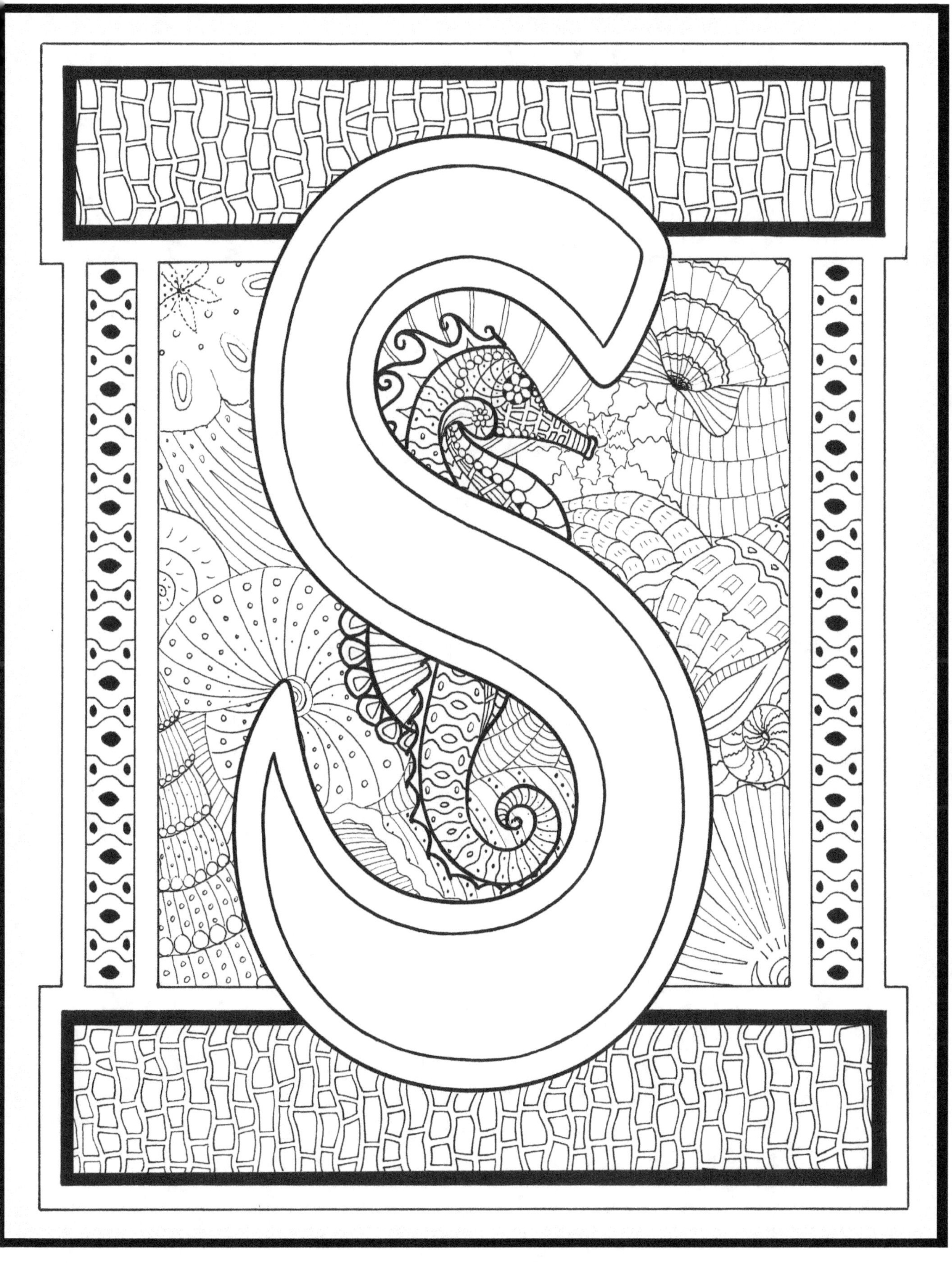

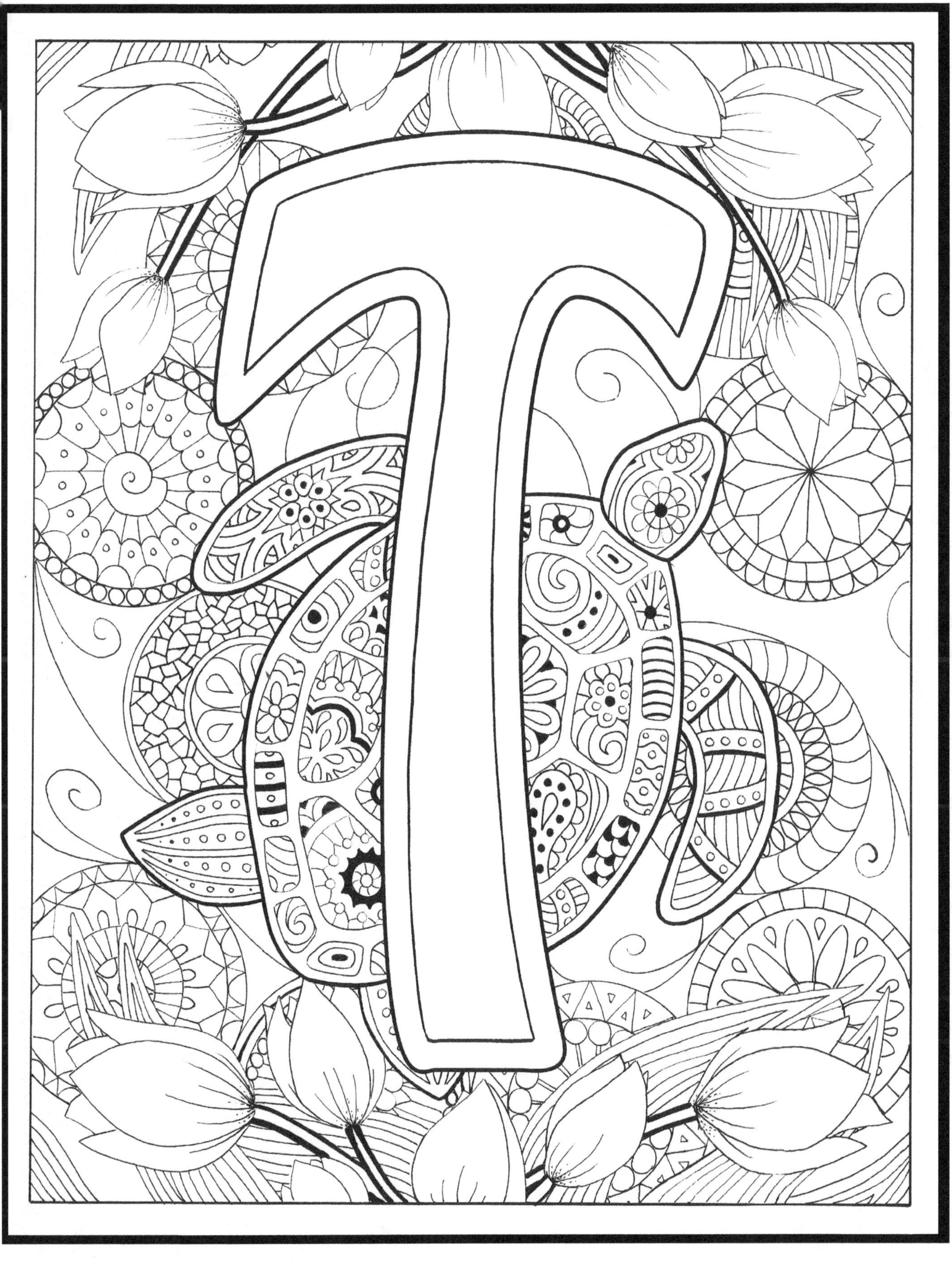

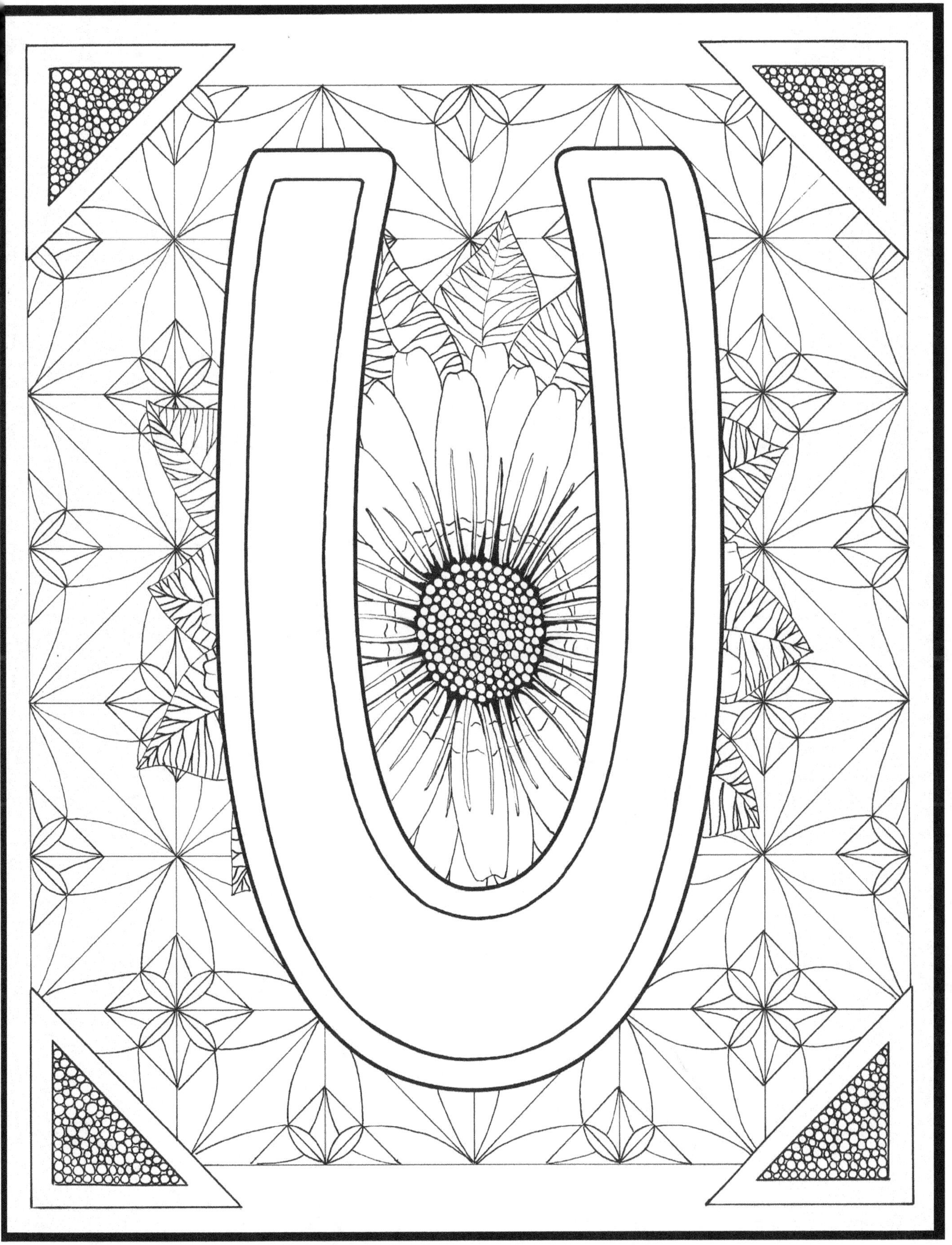

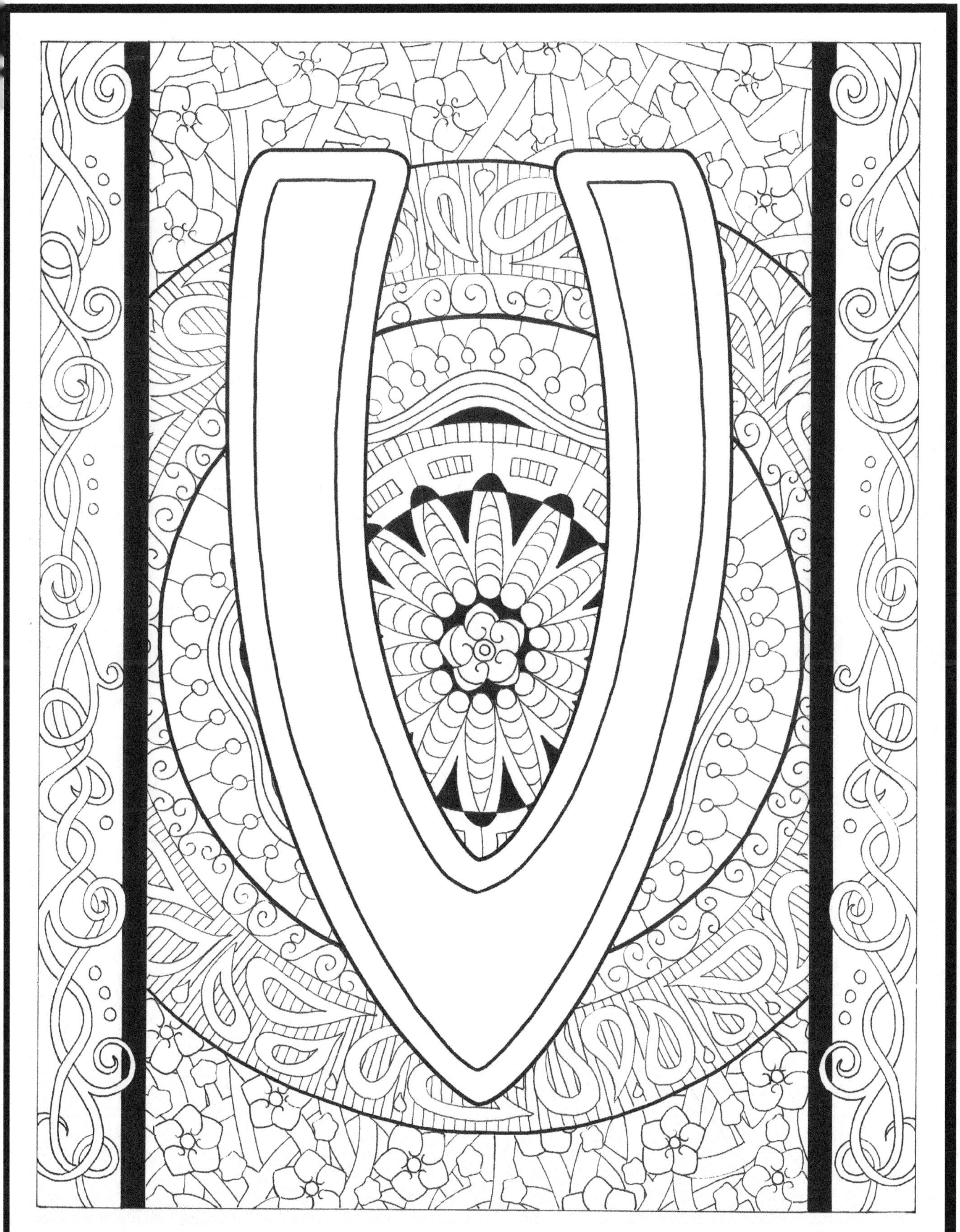

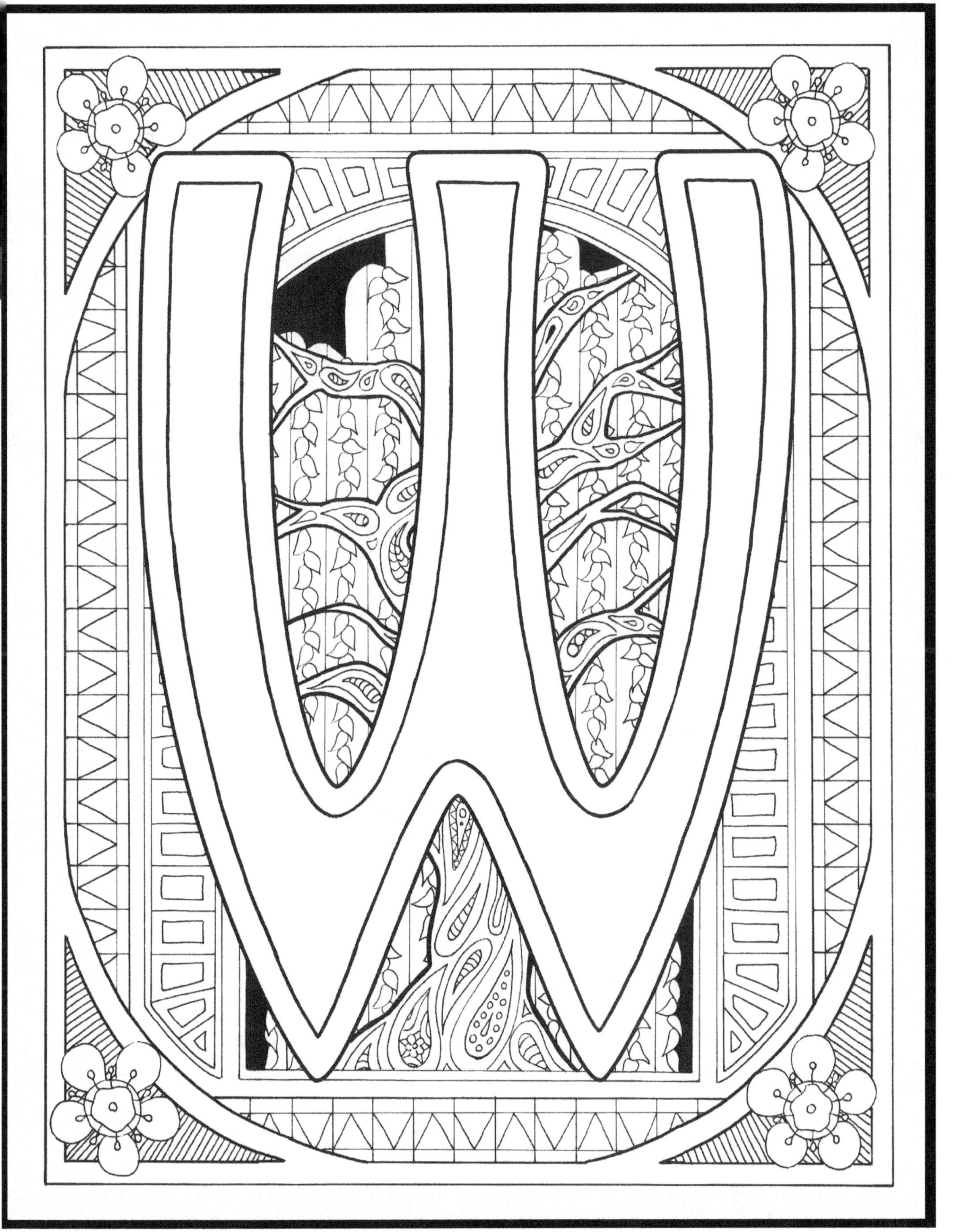

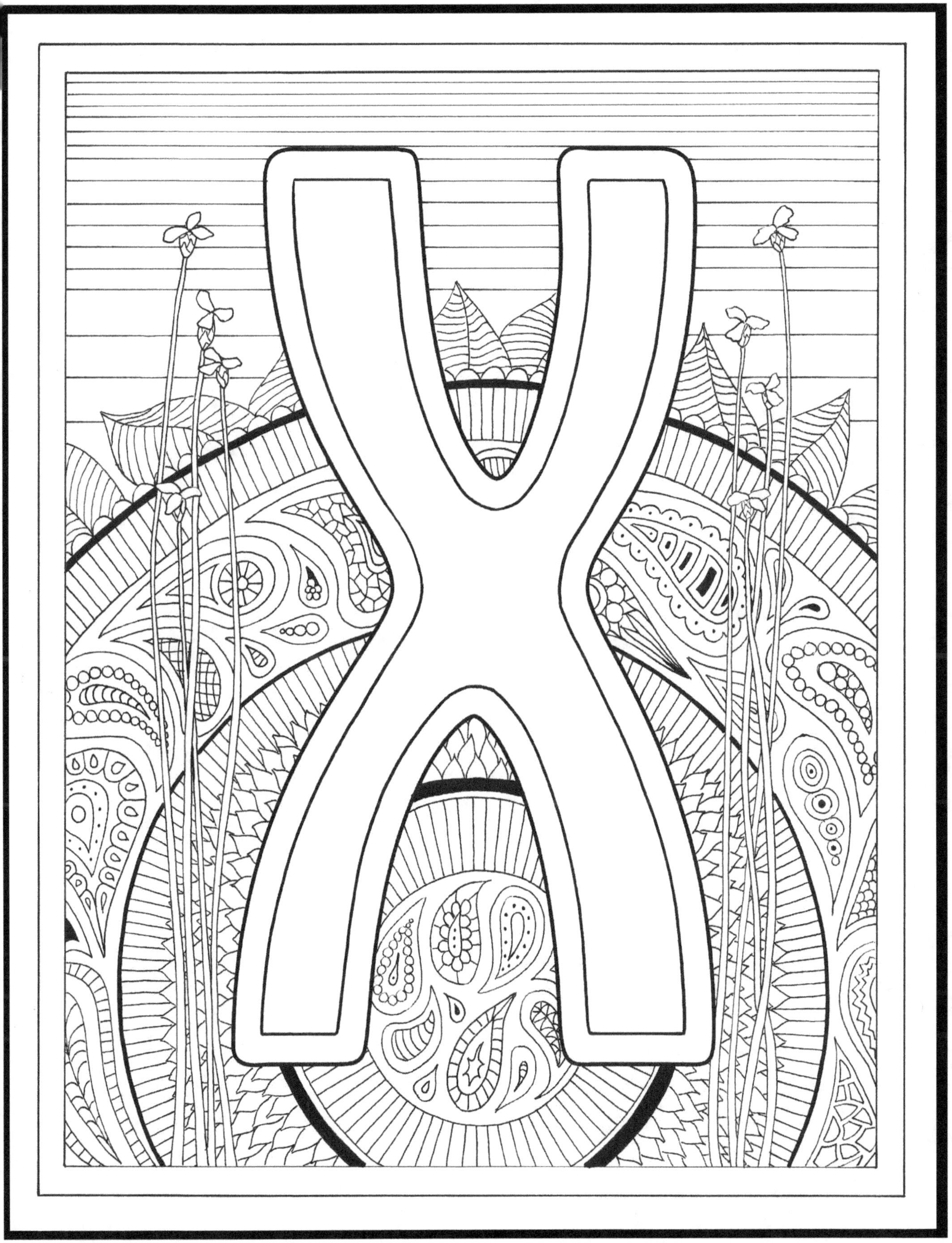

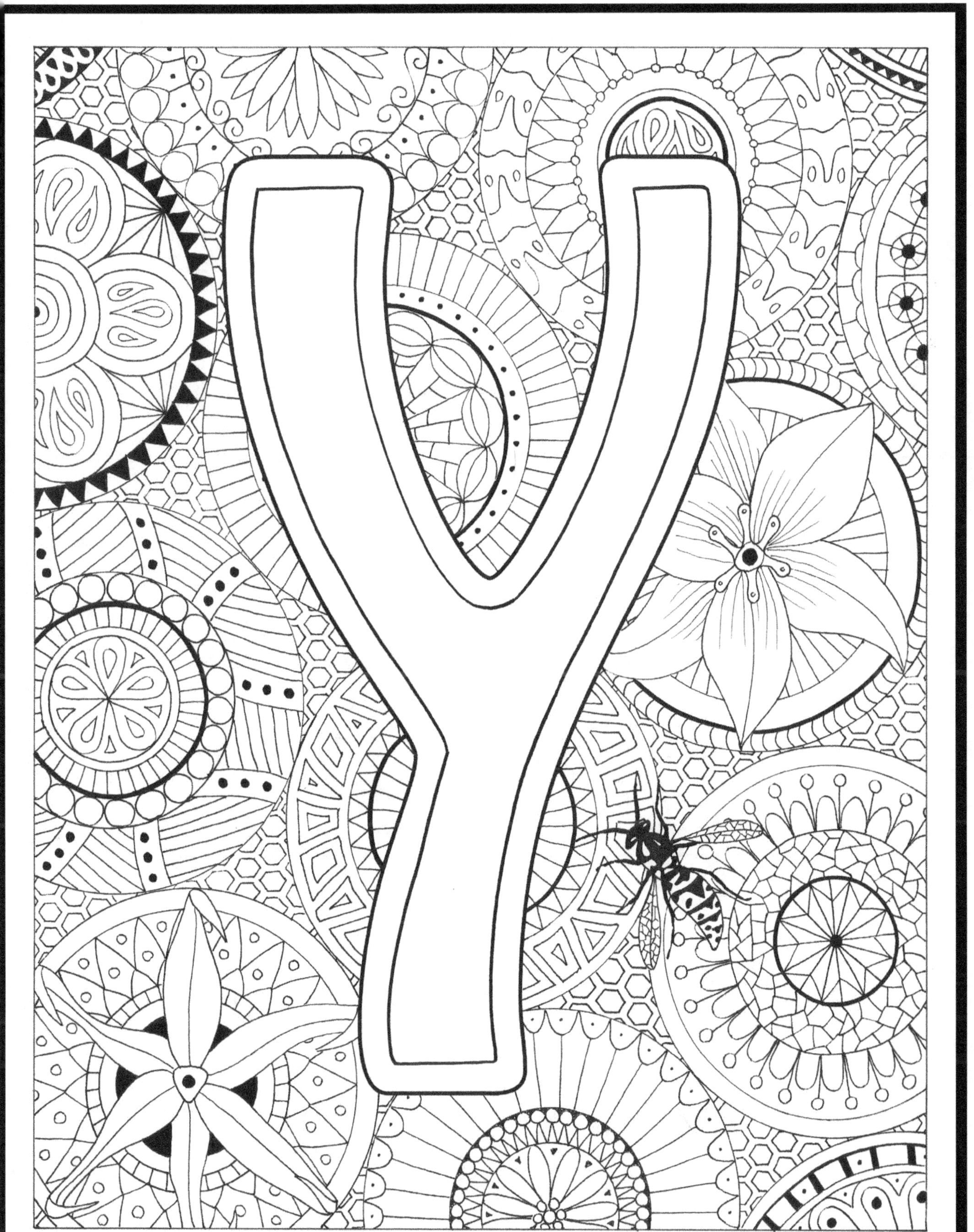

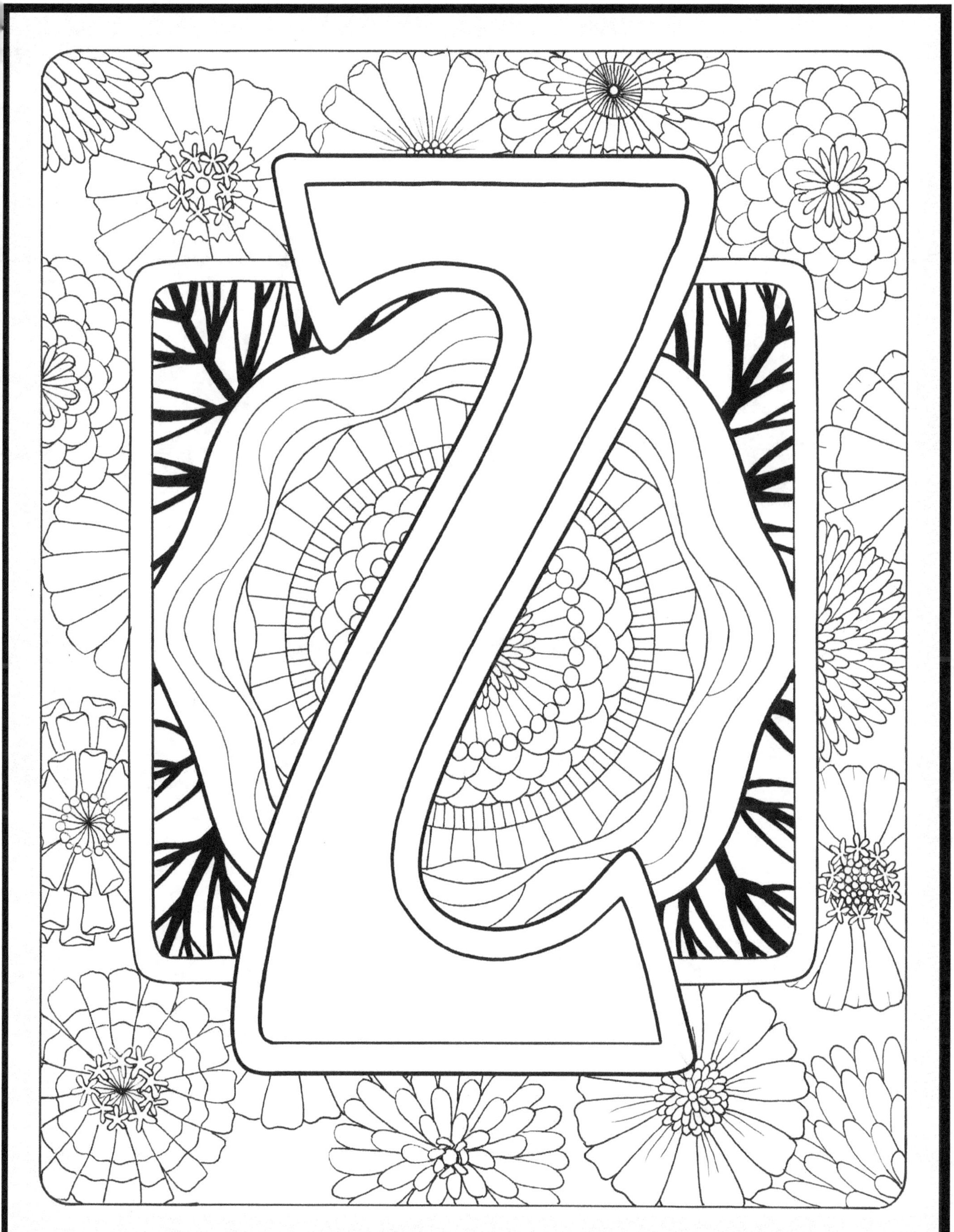

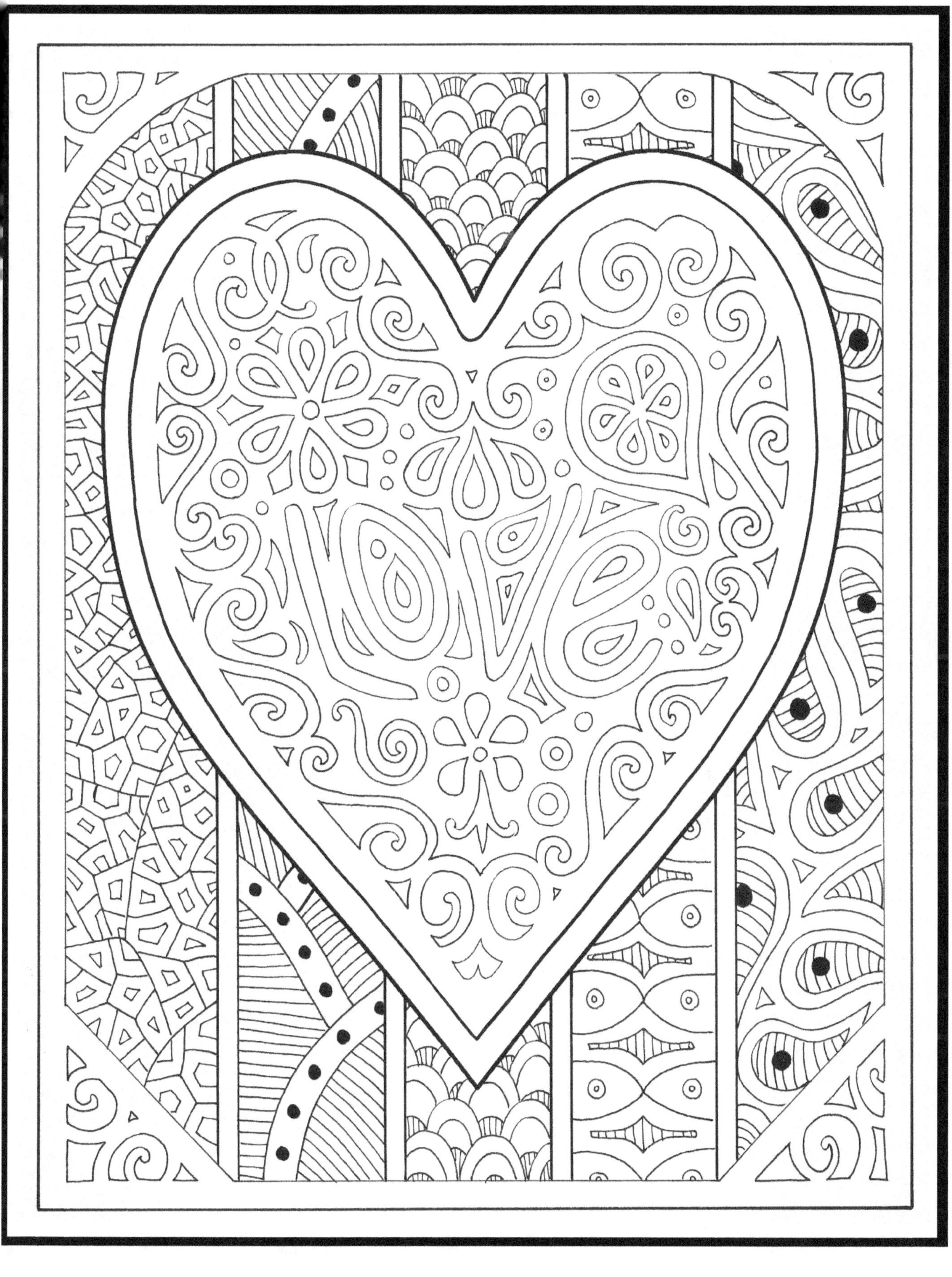
love

www.ingramcontent.com/pod-product-compliance
Lightning Source LLC
Chambersburg PA
CBHW080550190526
45169CB00007B/2711
* 9 7 8 1 5 3 0 6 9 0 2 8 2 *